All About
Seeds

by Melvin Berger
illustrated by Anna DiVito

SCHOLASTIC INC.

New York Toronto London Auckland Sydney

For Betty and Dan, with love
— M.B.

For Ann M. McCarthy and her dog Marty,
the urban gardeners
— A.D.

ISBN 0-590-44909-5

12 11 10 9 8 7 6 5 4 3 2   2 3 4 5 6 7/9

Printed in the U.S.A.   23

First Scholastic printing, March 1992

Seeds are all around you.

Bite into a peach or plum.
The big pit inside is a seed.
The little pits in apples and pears
are also seeds.

Look at a slice of tomato or cucumber.
Those little white bits you see are seeds.

Pick up an acorn or hickory nut.
Most nuts are seeds, too.
Break open a sunflower, daisy, or other flower.
Do you see the seeds packed together?

Walk into a supermarket.
You'll find peas and beans.
Rice and corn. Wheat and oats.
They're all seeds.

Seeds come from growing plants.
They are the beginnings of new plants.
Growing plants make lots and lots
of different kinds of seeds.

DO IT YOURSELF

Make a Seed Collection

Collect twelve different kinds of seeds.
Find seeds from fruits and vegetables,
from trees, from flowers, and from other plants.
How does each type of seed look and feel?
Take an empty egg carton.
Put each kind of seed in a different cup.
Put labels on the cups to help you remember
the plants your seeds came from.

Seeds come in many sizes.
Some seeds, like the coconut, are huge.
A coconut can be as big as your head.
It can weigh as much as a large sack of potatoes!

Some seeds are very, very small.
A strawberry has dozens and dozens
of tiny black seeds.
The seeds for an orchid flower are even smaller.
Millions of orchid seeds can fit onto a teaspoon!

Seeds can be round or pointed, smooth or rough,
curved or straight.
And seeds come in many different colors —
red, purple, white, orange, black.
Some even have stripes or spots!

All seeds look different.
Yet they're all the same in one way.
Inside each seed is a baby plant!

It's easy to see the baby plant in some seeds.
Lima beans, for example, are the seeds
of the lima bean plant.
And inside each lima bean is a baby plant.

The Inside of a
Lima Bean

DO IT YOURSELF

Can You Find the Baby Plant?

Buy a package of dried (not frozen) lima beans
in the supermarket.
Soak a few beans in water overnight.
Take them out of the water.
Slip off their outer coats with your fingers.
Then split open the beans.
Look inside. Do you see the baby plants?

Seeds do not grow if they are kept dry.
But when they are wet the seeds split open.
The baby plants start to grow.
Each plant sends out a green shoot called
a seedling.

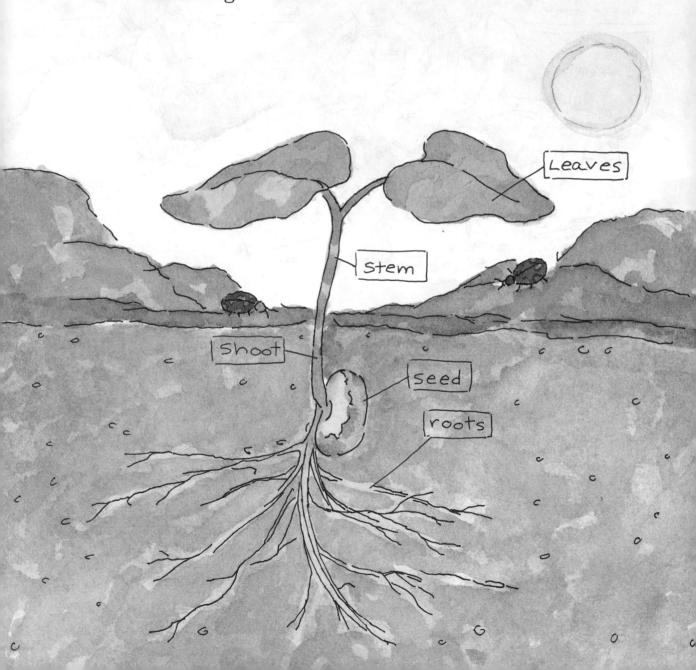

DO IT YOURSELF

Seeds Need Water

Get six dry lima beans, two paper towels,
and two saucers.
Fold each paper towel in half.
Then fold each one in half again.
Lay a folded towel on each saucer.
In one saucer add enough water to make
the whole paper towel wet.
Place three lima beans on that wet towel.
In the other saucer place three lima beans
on the *dry* towel.
Set this saucer next to the first one.
In a couple of days you'll see seedlings
in the wet saucer.
The dry saucer has no seedlings at all.

Seeds cannot grow without water.
But seeds also need to be warm.
When seeds are warm, the baby plants
start to grow.

DO IT YOURSELF

Seeds Need Warmth

Take six lima beans.
Fill two paper cups nearly full with soil.
Put three seeds in each cup.

fill to
here
with
soil

Push them down until the soil covers
the first joint of your thumb.
Spread the soil over the seeds.
Add enough water to each cup to make
a small puddle on top.
Set one cup in a warm place.
Set the other in the refrigerator.
Add a teaspoon of water to each cup every day
to keep the soil damp.
In a few days you'll see tiny seedlings
in the warm cup.
The cold cup will not have any seedlings at all.

Seeds need water to grow.
And they need to be warm.
But they need something more.
Seeds need food to grow.

Most seeds contain food for the baby plant.
In the lima bean the food is in the two halves
of the bean.
The baby plant uses that food to start growing.

I ♡ EARTH

But soon the food is all used up.
How does the plant get more food?

Plants can make their own food.
But first, most plants must be growing in soil.

DO IT YOURSELF

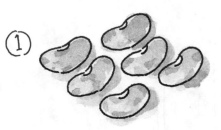

Plants Need Soil

Take two paper cups and six lima beans.
Fill one cup nearly full with soil.
Add enough water to make a small puddle on top.
Stuff a wet paper towel into the other cup.
Press three lima beans into the soil.
Push the seeds down until the soil covers
the first joint of your thumb.
Press three lima beans the same distance
into the wet towel.
Place both cups in a sunny place.
Every day add a teaspoon of water to both cups.
In a few days, you'll see seedlings in both cups.

Leave the cups in the sunny place.
Keep watering the soil and the towel.
After a week or so, the seedlings in the soil
will still be growing.
But the seedlings in the wet towel
will be drooping.
They have used up all the food in the seed.
The soil gives plants the water and food
they need.
To keep growing, plants need water, warmth,
and soil.

(2)

fill to here with soil

(3)

(4)

(5)

first joint

(6)

(7)

soil

paper towel

(8)

SOIL

paper towel

Most plants that grow in soil have roots, a stem
and leaves.
The roots always point down.
The stem and leaves always point up.
They face the sun.
Plants face up because they must have sunlight
to grow.

DO IT YOURSELF ①

<u>Plants Need Sunlight</u>

Take two paper cups and six lima beans.
Fill both cups nearly to the top with soil.
Put three seeds in each cup.
Push them down until the soil covers
the first joint of your thumb.
Add enough water to each cup to make
a small puddle on top.
Place one cup on a bright, sunny windowsill.
Place the other in a dark closet.
Every day add a teaspoon of water to each cup.
In a few days you'll see seedlings in both cups.

Leave the cups where they are.
Continue to water the plants.
In a few more days the plants in the sunlight
will be big and strong.
But the plants in the closet will stop growing
and die.
Plants need sunshine.
Without light, the leaves can't make food
for the plant.

The stem and leaves push up to get light
from the sun.
At the same time, the roots push down
to get water and food from the soil.

But what happens if you plant a seed upside down?

DO IT YOURSELF

Can Roots Grow Up? Can Stems Grow Down?

Take a paper towel.
Fold it in half.
Then fold it in half again the same way.
Wet the towel and form it into a ring.
Place the wet towel ring inside a short,
wide drinking glass.
Press the towel against the sides of the glass.
Get eight lima beans.
Slip the beans between the towel and the glass.
Place the lima beans in all different directions.
Set the glass in a warm place.
Add a tablespoon of water to the bottom
of the glass each day to keep the towel damp.
Soon you'll see stems and roots coming
from the beans.
Which way do the roots grow?
Which way do the stems grow?

wet
towel
ring

The roots always grow down.
They hold the plants down in the ground.

Roots mostly stay in one place.
Yet seeds from their plants can spread
far and wide.
How do seeds travel?

Seeds travel in different ways.
When violet and pansy flowers open, their seeds
escape into the air.
The wind blows the seeds of maple and ash trees
long distances.

Birds also scatter seeds.
Finches and sparrows crack the hard shells
of seeds.
The seeds fall to earth and start new plants.

Animals, such as squirrels, are good
seed spreaders.
Often, they dig holes and hide nuts.
But sometimes they forget where the nuts
are buried.
And these nuts stay in the ground.
Coconut trees often grow near the sea.
The coconuts fall.
Some roll into the ocean and float away.
They may wash up on another shore and get
buried in the sand.

Have you ever eaten a fruit — and tossed
the seeds on the ground?
Have you ever blown on the fluffy white ball
of a dandelion plant?
Have you ever pulled burrs off your clothes
and tossed them aside?
Perhaps some of these seeds will grow
into plants.
You, too, may have helped to move seeds around.

Any seed, given enough water, warmth, good soil,
and sunlight, may grow into a new plant.
Sometimes the plant starts to grow right away.
Other times it takes a long while to get started.

Once it begins to grow, the plant sends
down roots.
It pushes up its stem and leaves.
Soon the new plant looks like the plant
the seed came from.

In time, the plant begins to make seeds
of its own.
The seeds travel or are planted in the soil.
And the whole cycle starts all over again.

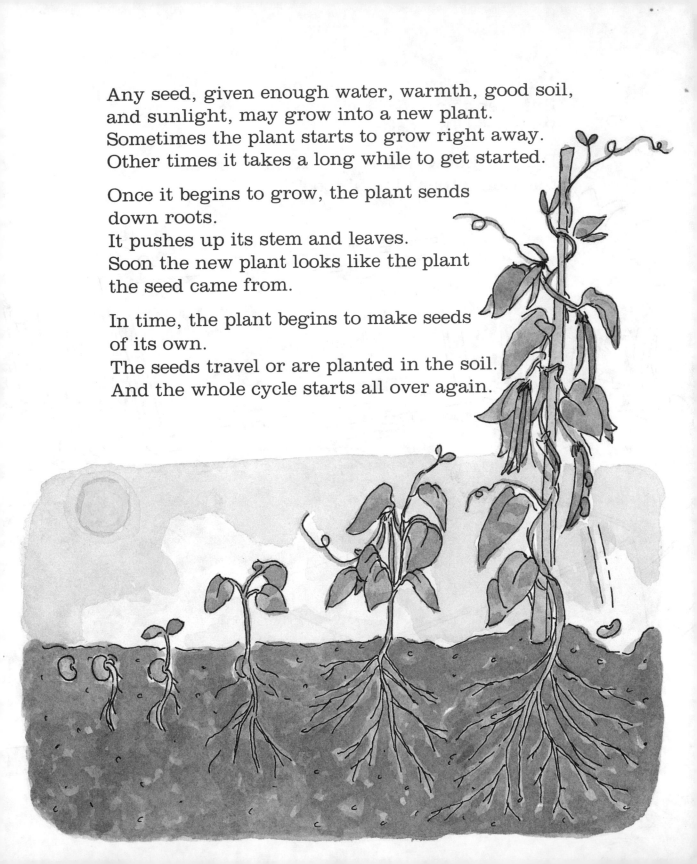

Many seeds grow into new plants.
But even more seeds are used just as they are.
People eat them as food.

Did you know that people eat more seeds
than any other kind of food?

Americans love bread and macaroni made from wheat.
In China and Japan people eat noodles
and other foods made from rice.
Corn is the favorite food in Mexico
and many other countries.
Wheat, rice, corn — they are all seeds!

Granola is a delicious dish that is made
from several different seeds.
Many people eat granola for breakfast
or at snacktime.
You can prepare it at home.

DO IT YOURSELF

Make Some Granola

1 cup uncooked oats
½ cup chopped nuts
½ cup sesame seeds
½ cup sunflower seeds
½ cup shredded coconut
½ cup wheat germ
¼ cup brown sugar, packed
¼ teaspoon salt

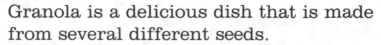

Place the oats and the nuts in a large,
heavy frying pan.
Put the frying pan on the stove.
Ask an adult to turn the heat to medium-low.
Set a timer for five minutes.
Carefully stir the oats and nuts.
After the five minutes, add the sesame seeds,
sunflower seeds, coconut, and wheat germ.
Set the timer for ten more minutes. Stir.
After ten minutes, sprinkle in the brown sugar
and salt.
Set the timer and stir for three more minutes.
Remove from heat. Let it cool.

5 minutes

10 minutes

3 minutes

As you eat the granola, think about all
the different seeds it contains.
And remember that:

- Seeds come from growing plants.
- All seeds contain baby plants.
- Many seeds grow into new plants.
- But even more seeds are used to feed billions
  of people all over the world!